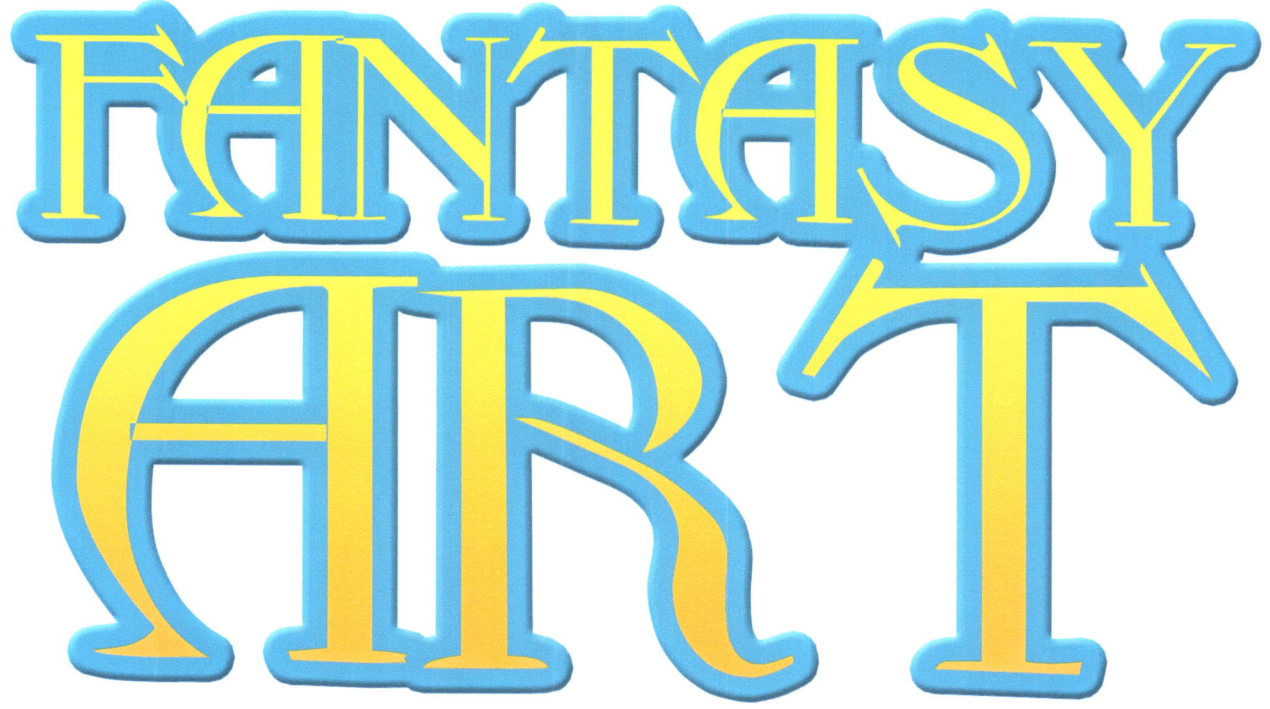

FANTASY ART

A KID-TO-KID COLORING BOOK

MAYA ESMAIL

Printed in the United States of America

Design and Illustration Support: Daniel Yeager (Nu-Image Design)

First Printing, 2017

ISBN-13:978-0692900703 (Rainbow Sky Publishing)

ISBN-10:0692900705

About Maya

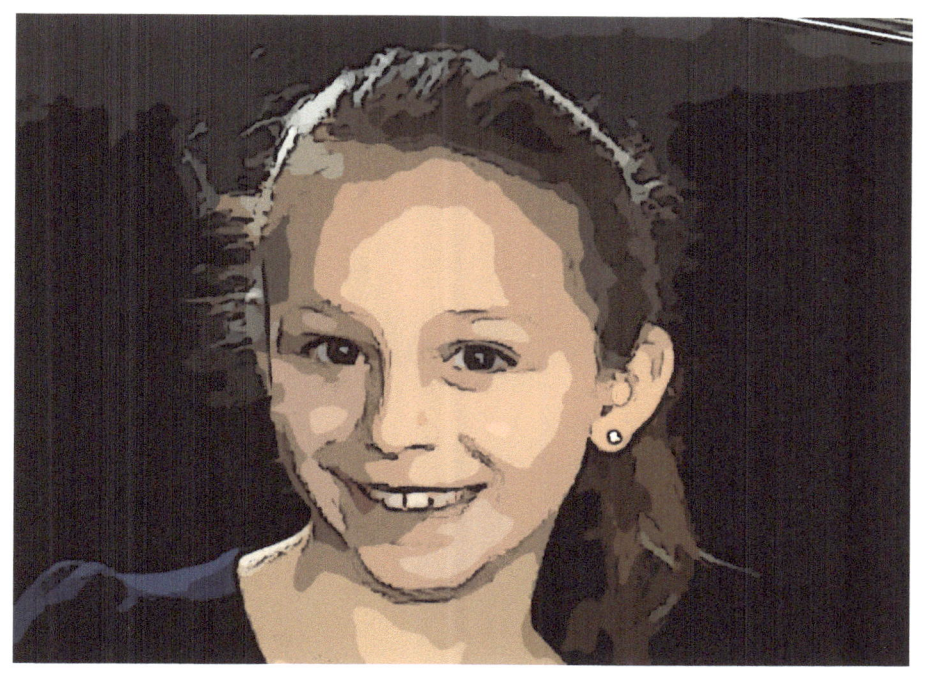

Maya lives in California with her mom, dad, her sister Anya, her bunny Nutella and Momo (her puppy dog). She loves to draw and write. She is in second grade. She loves art, fantasy characters and books. When she is not drawing or reading, she enjoys being silly with her sister, chatting with her friends or riding horses.

Introduction

This coloring book was imagined and created by 7 year old Maya to raise money for those that have less because she dreams of a better colorful world for all.

Maya loves to draw every day. Many of the characters in this book have a name and a story that Maya imagined.

There is Rainbow Sky who thought she had lost her mother but reunites with her in the rainbow sky.

Cheetah Girl, Unicorn Girl and Cat Girl live in an orphanage in the wild and have to work hard every day to survive. But they never lose their spirit and special powers.

Meet Midnight who spreads her love of animals.

Roje is a strong warrior who lives in the Kingdom of Fantasy.

All of them are special to Maya and she invites you to create your own story around them.

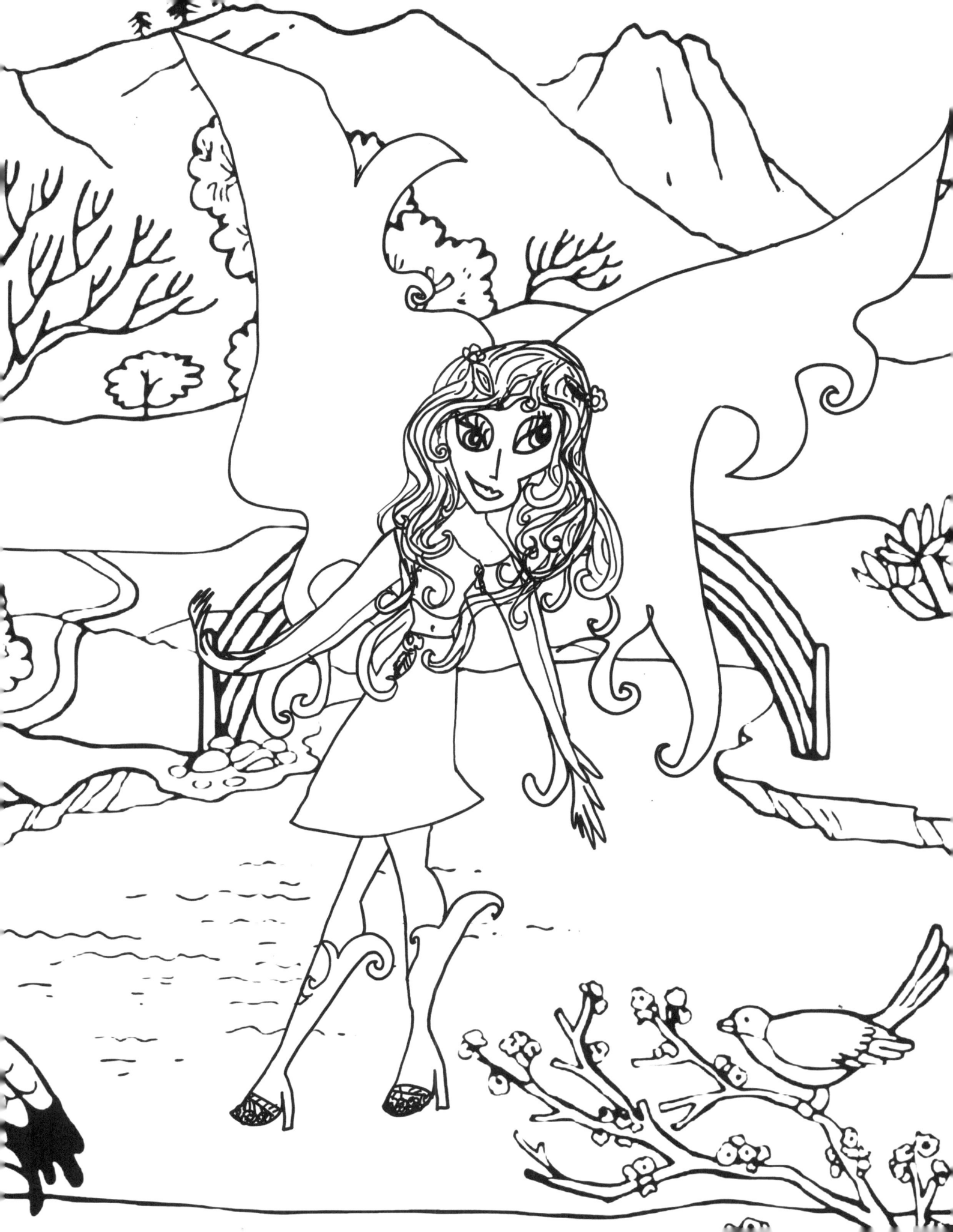

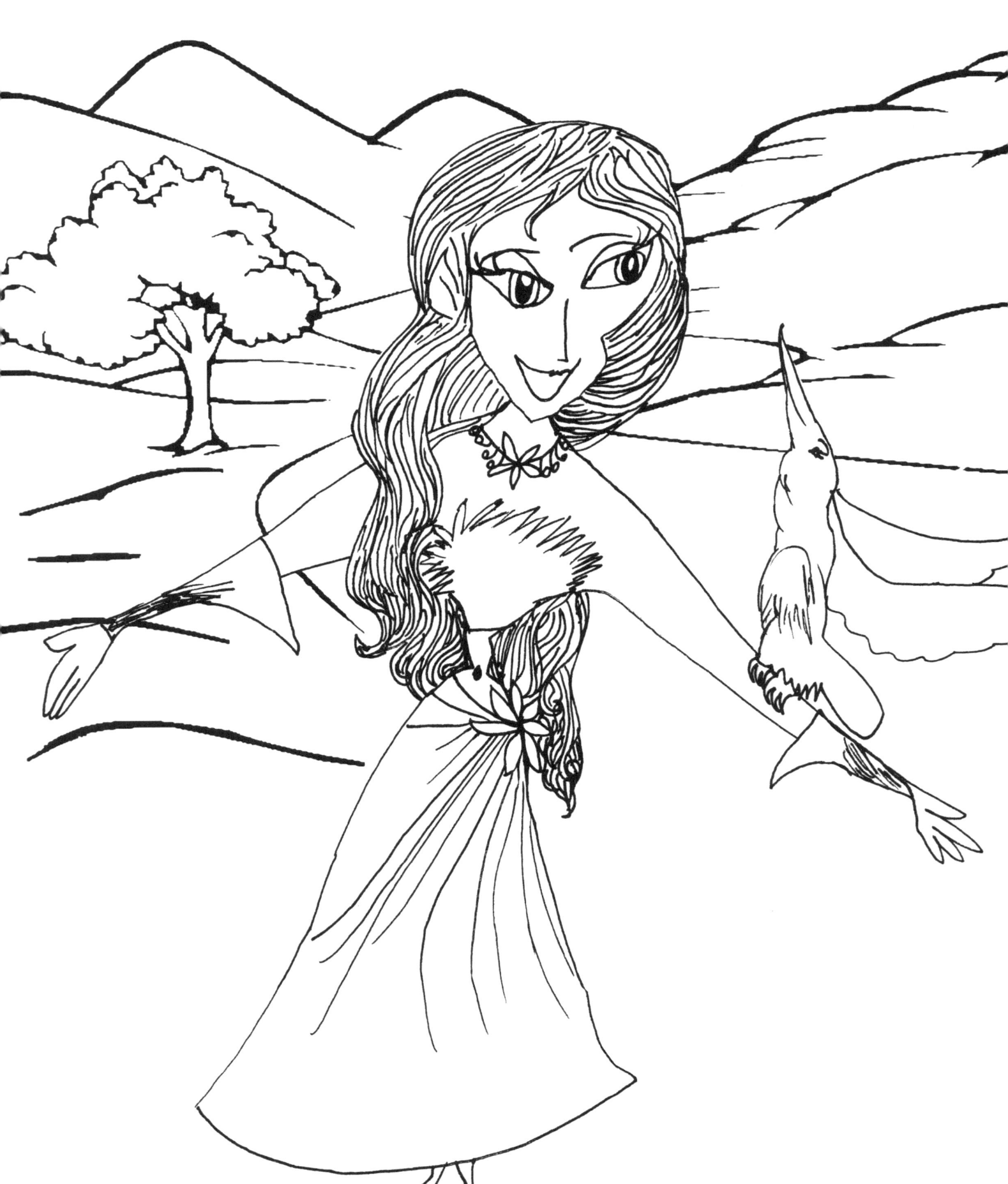

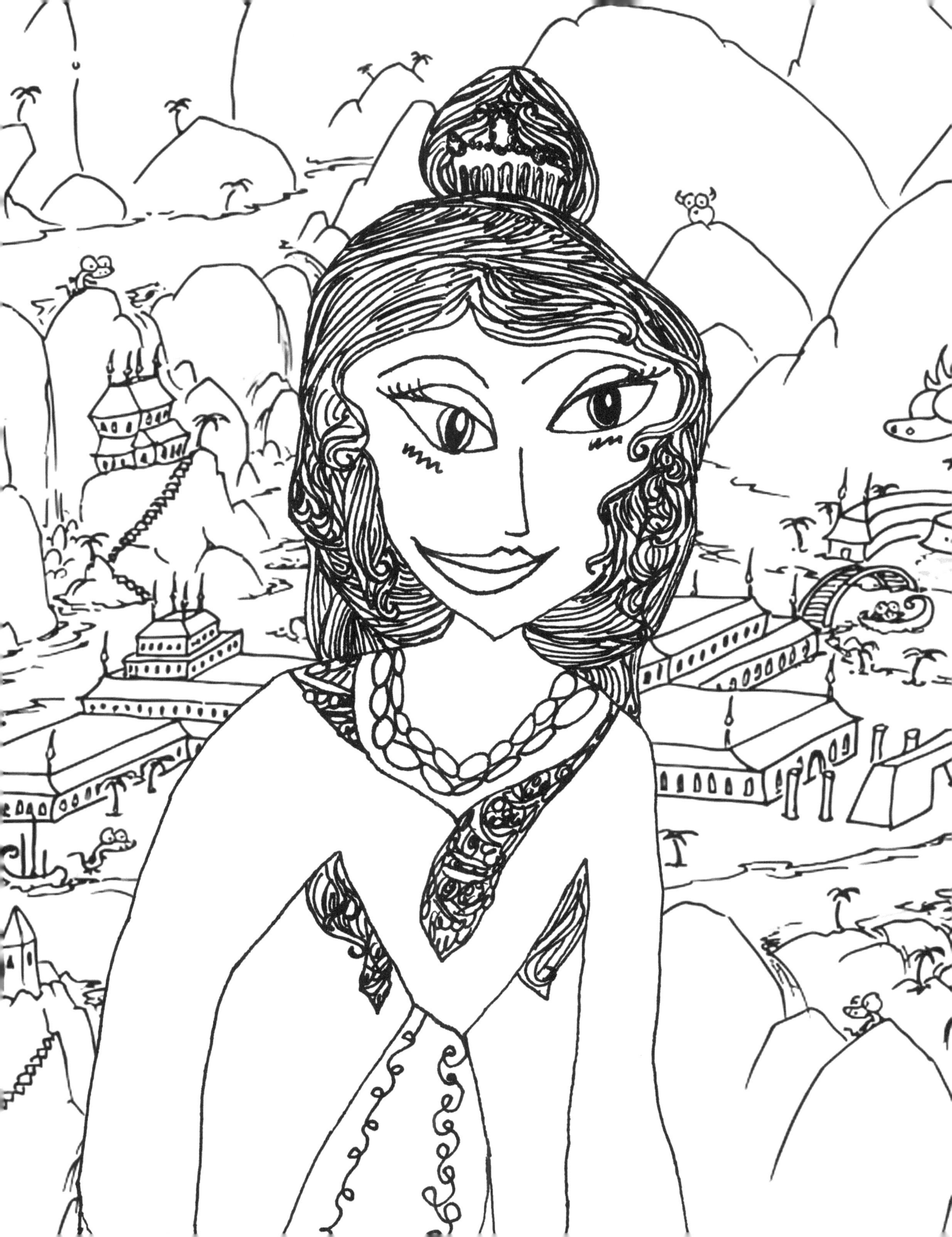

Unicorn Girl

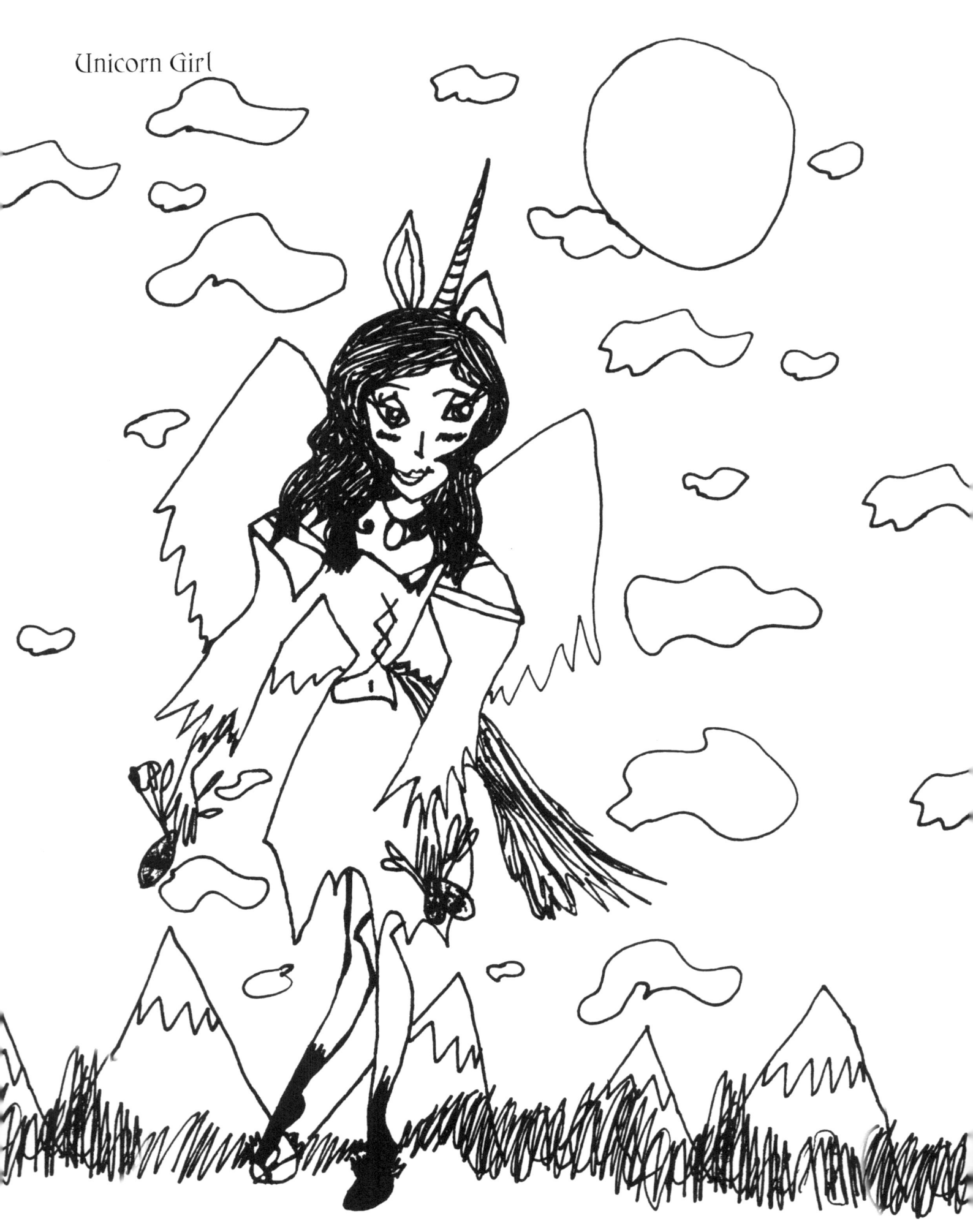

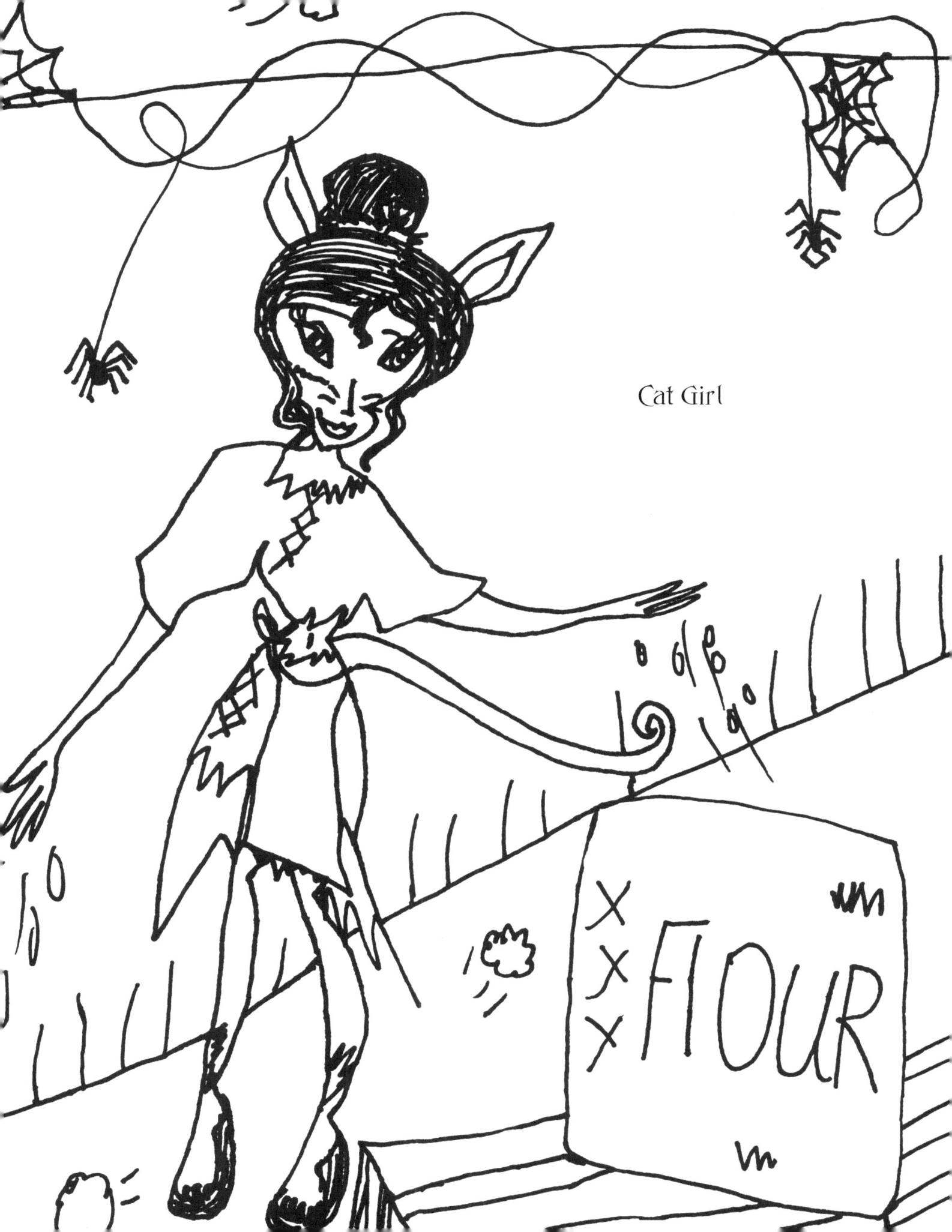

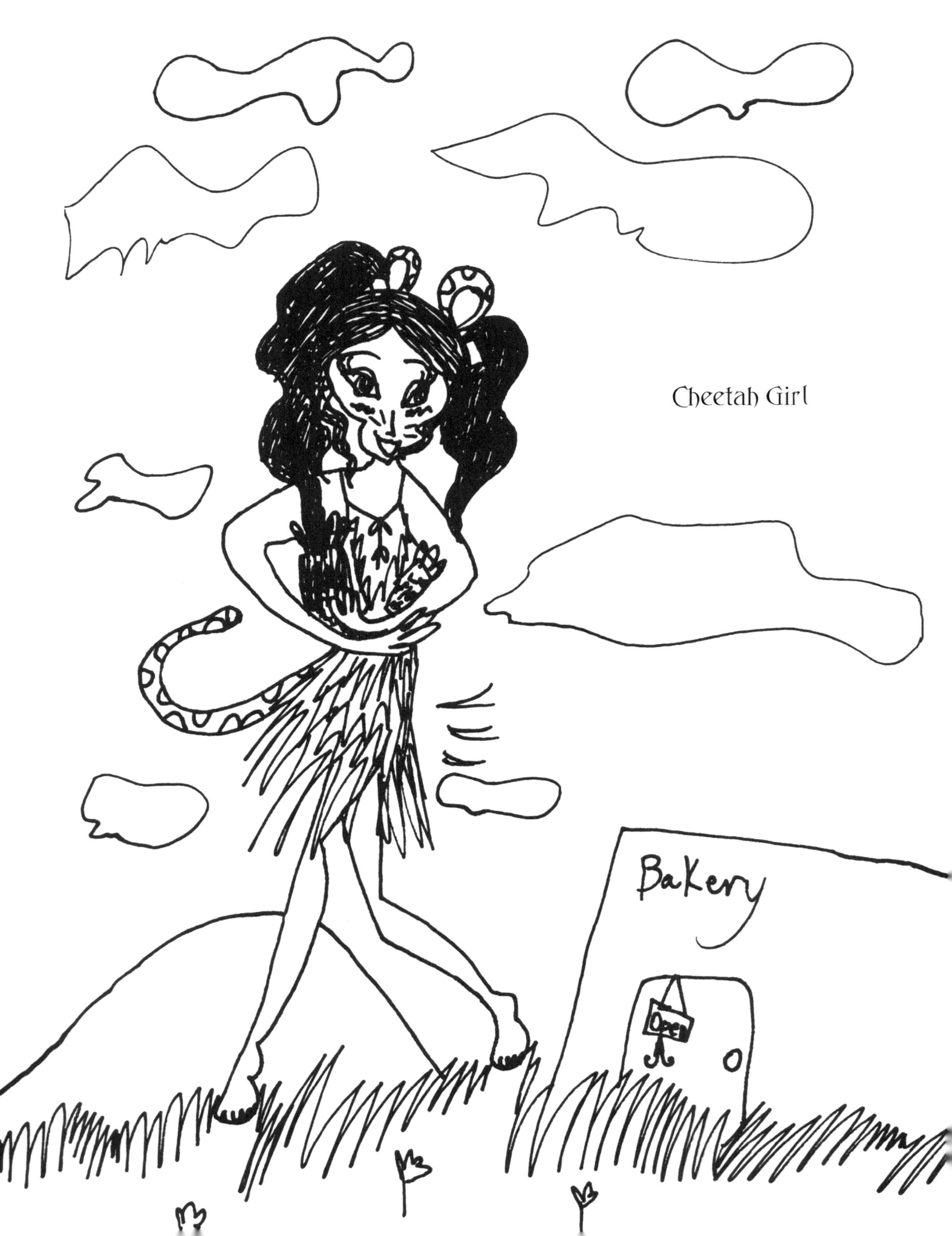

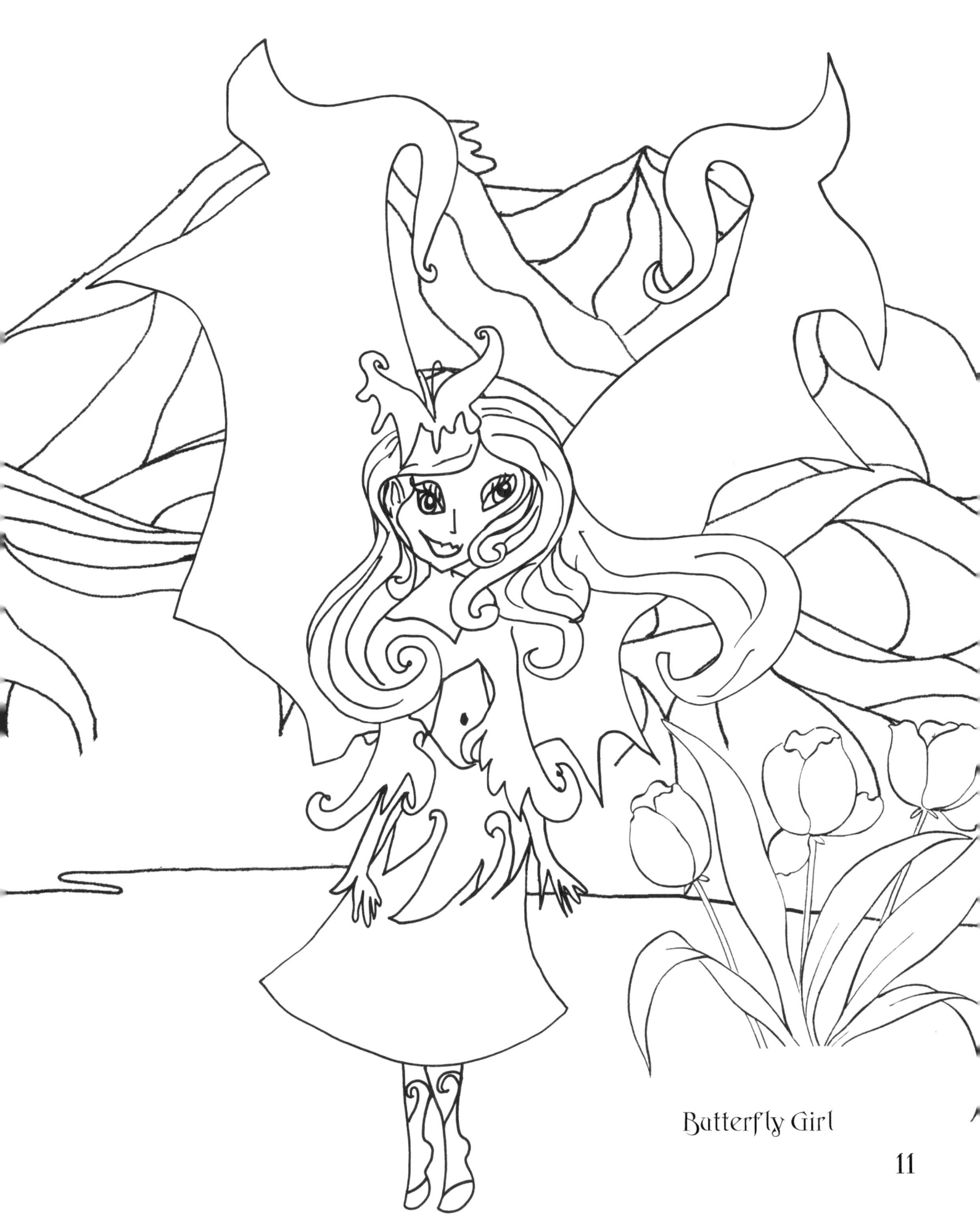

Butterfly Girl

11

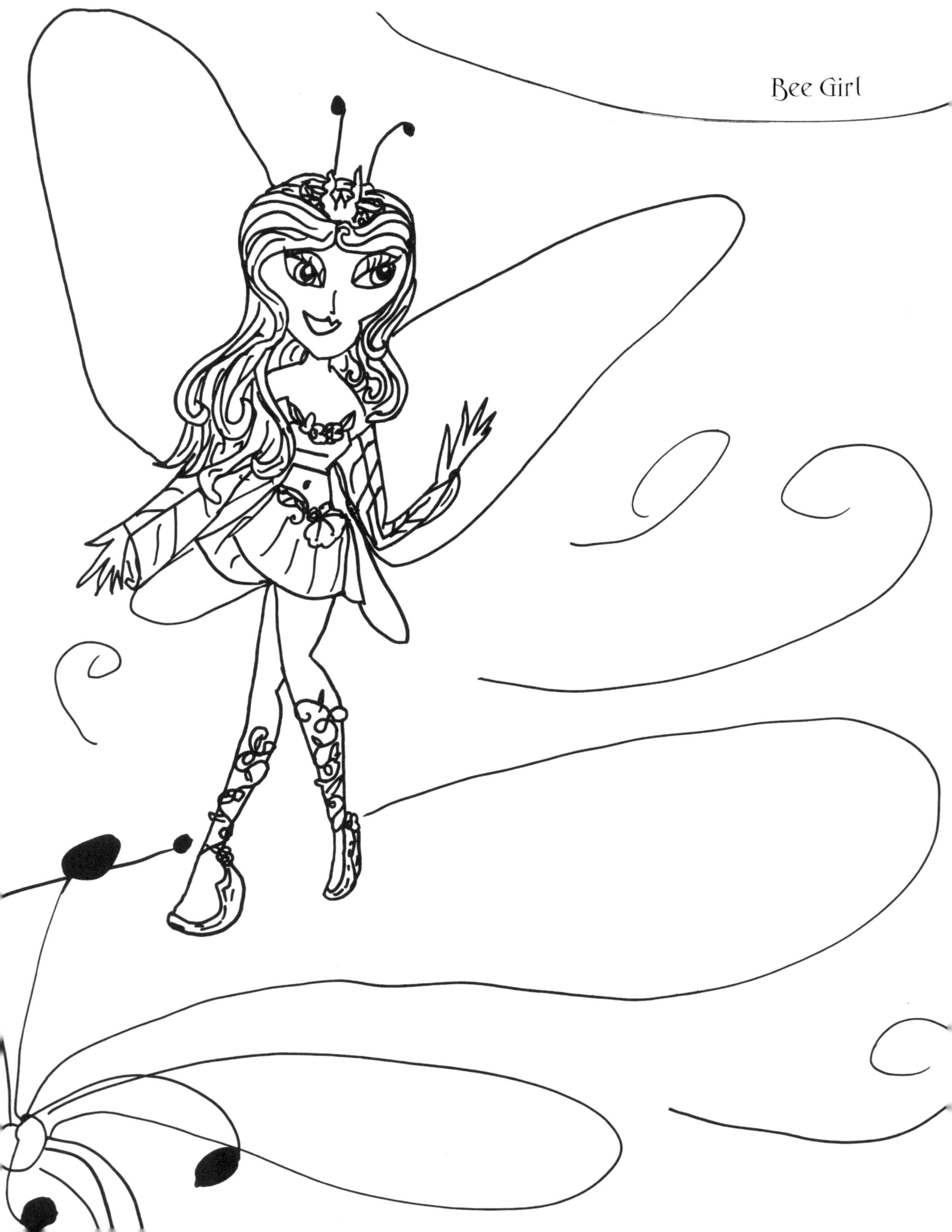

Bee Girl

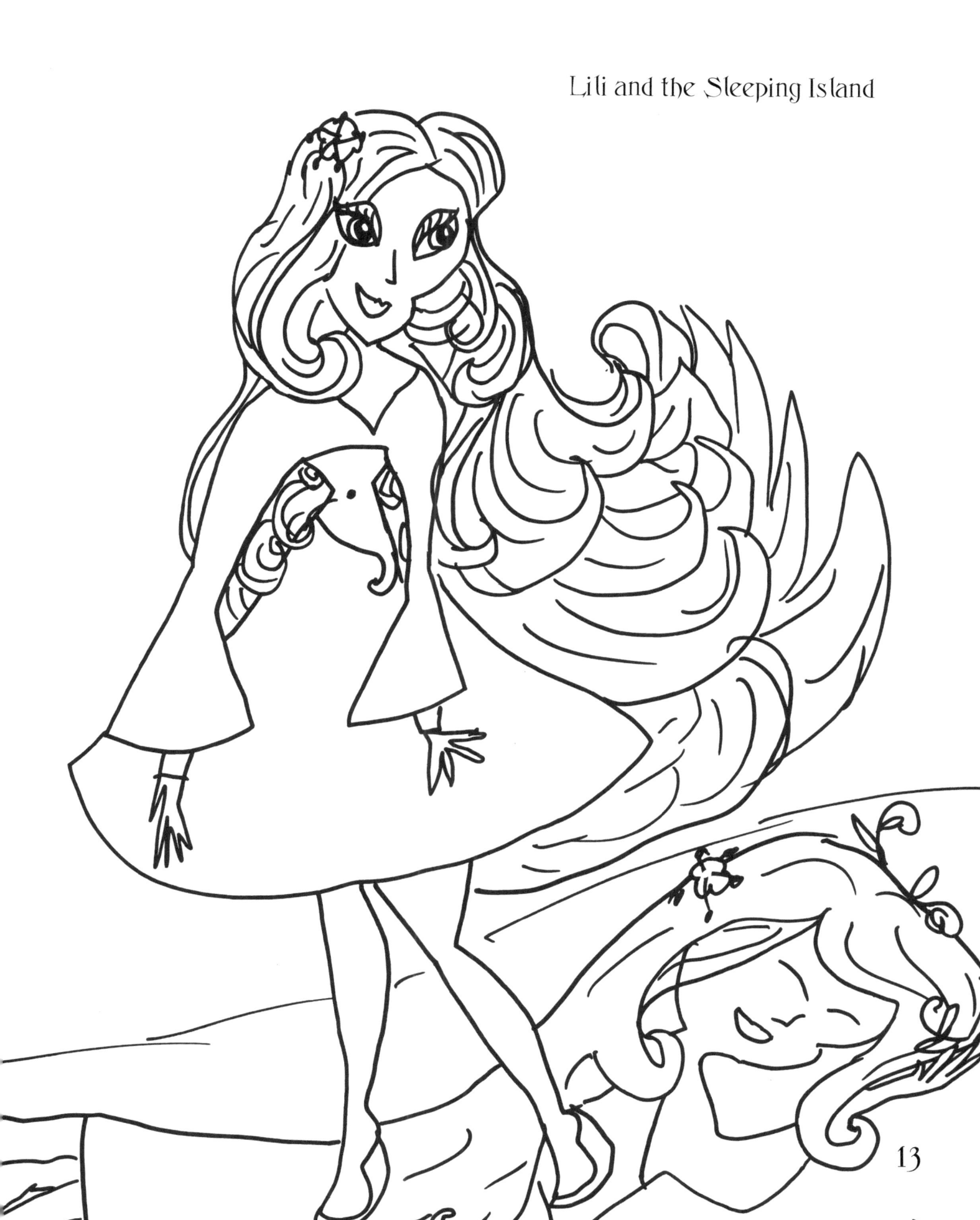

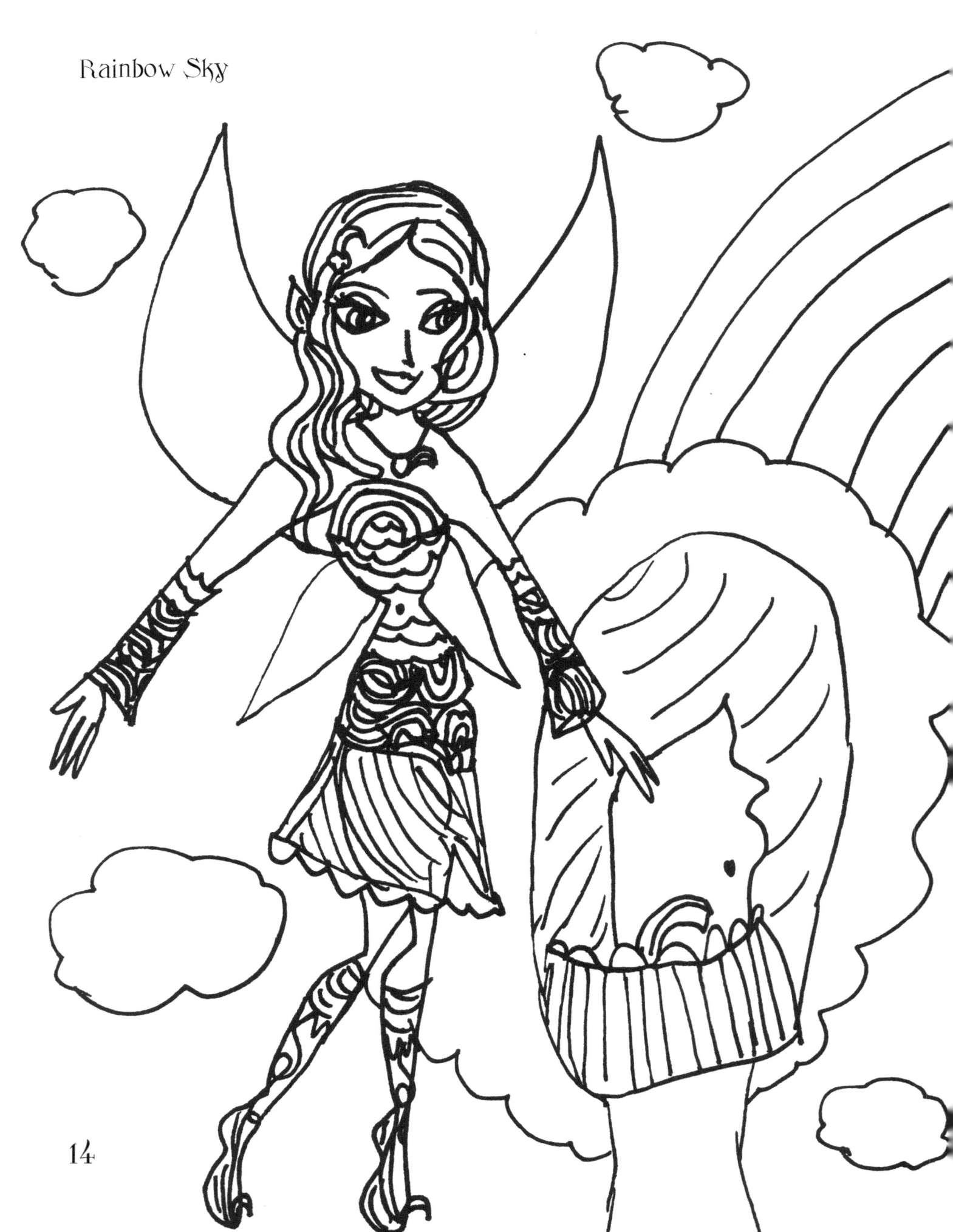

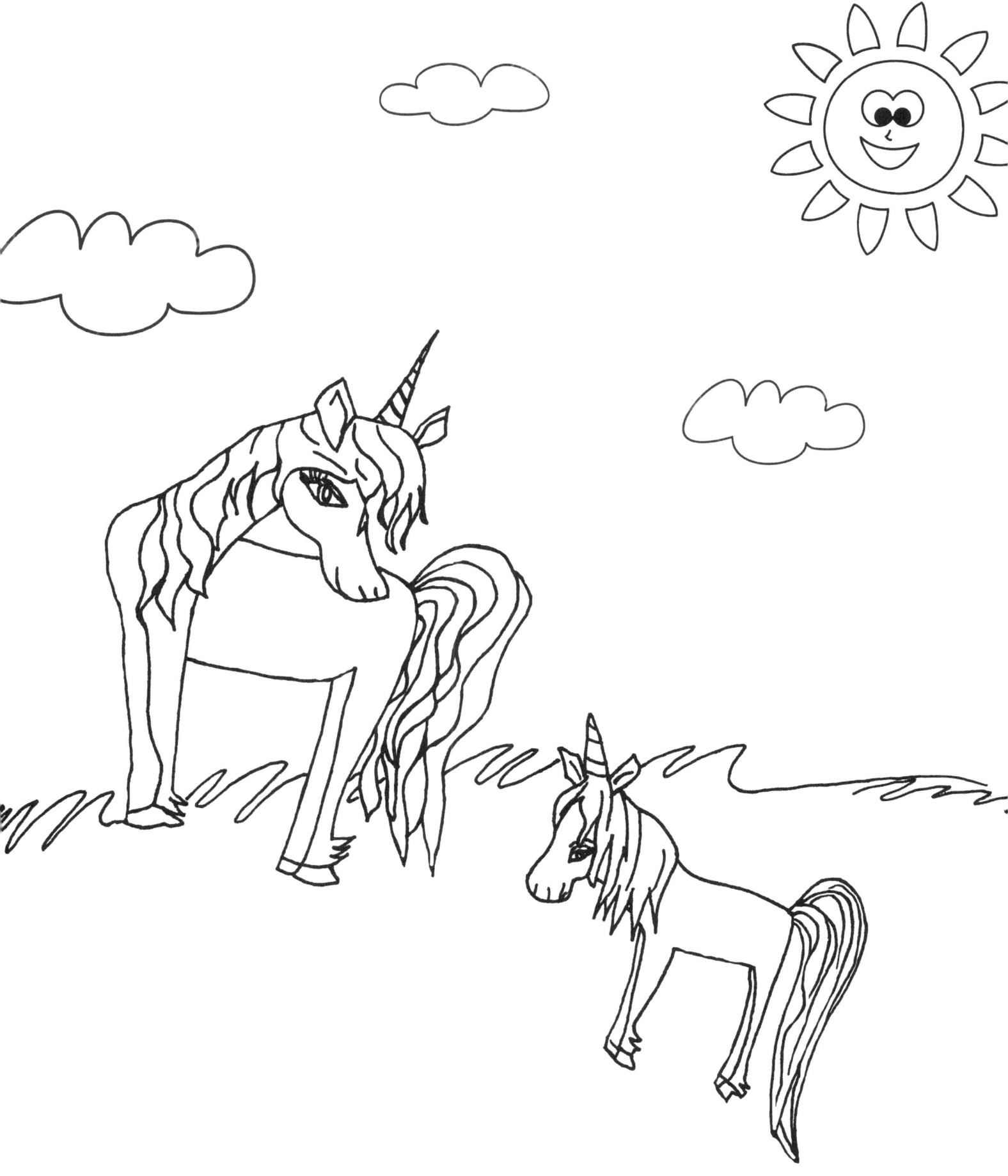

Emma

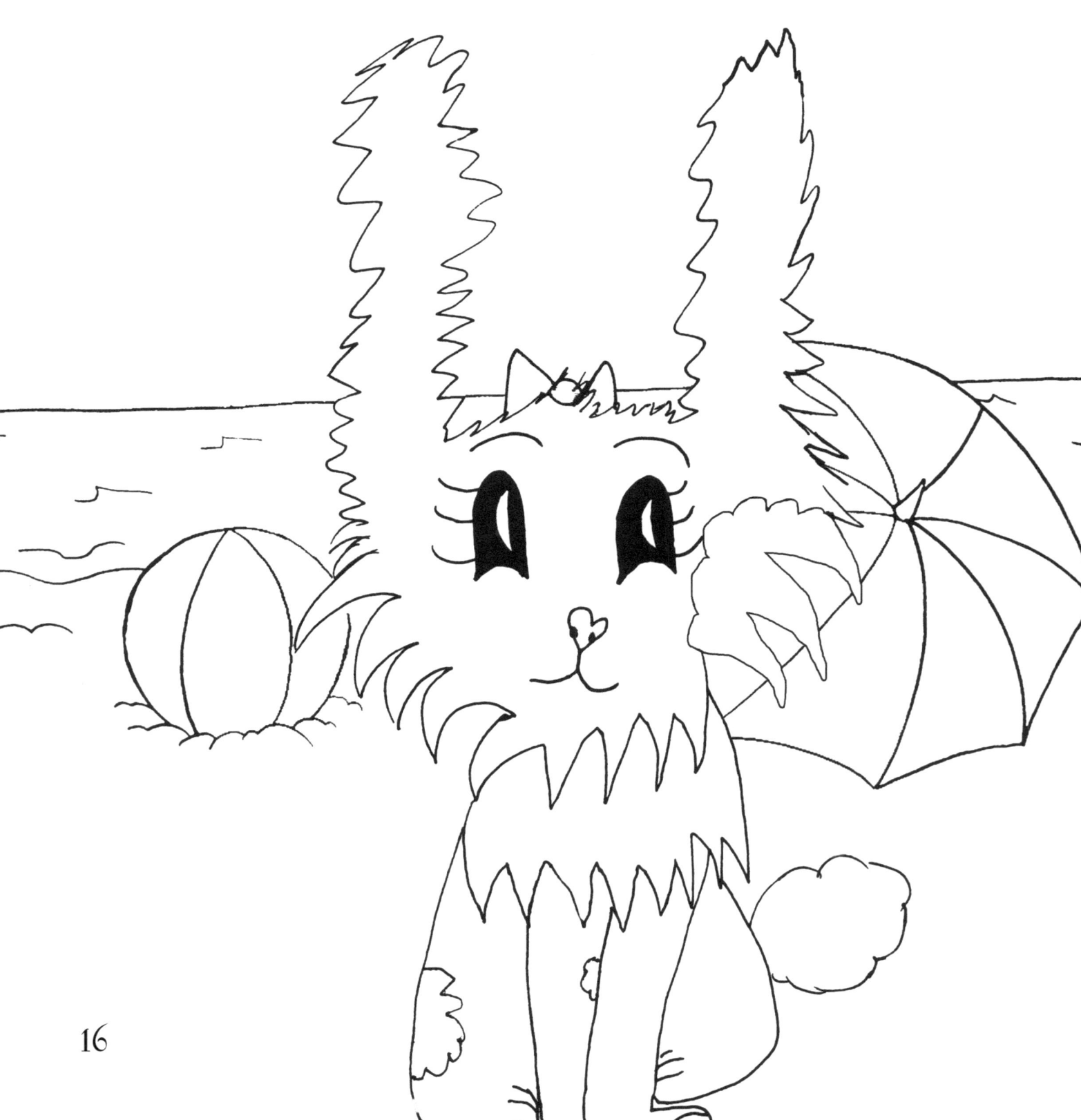

Momo

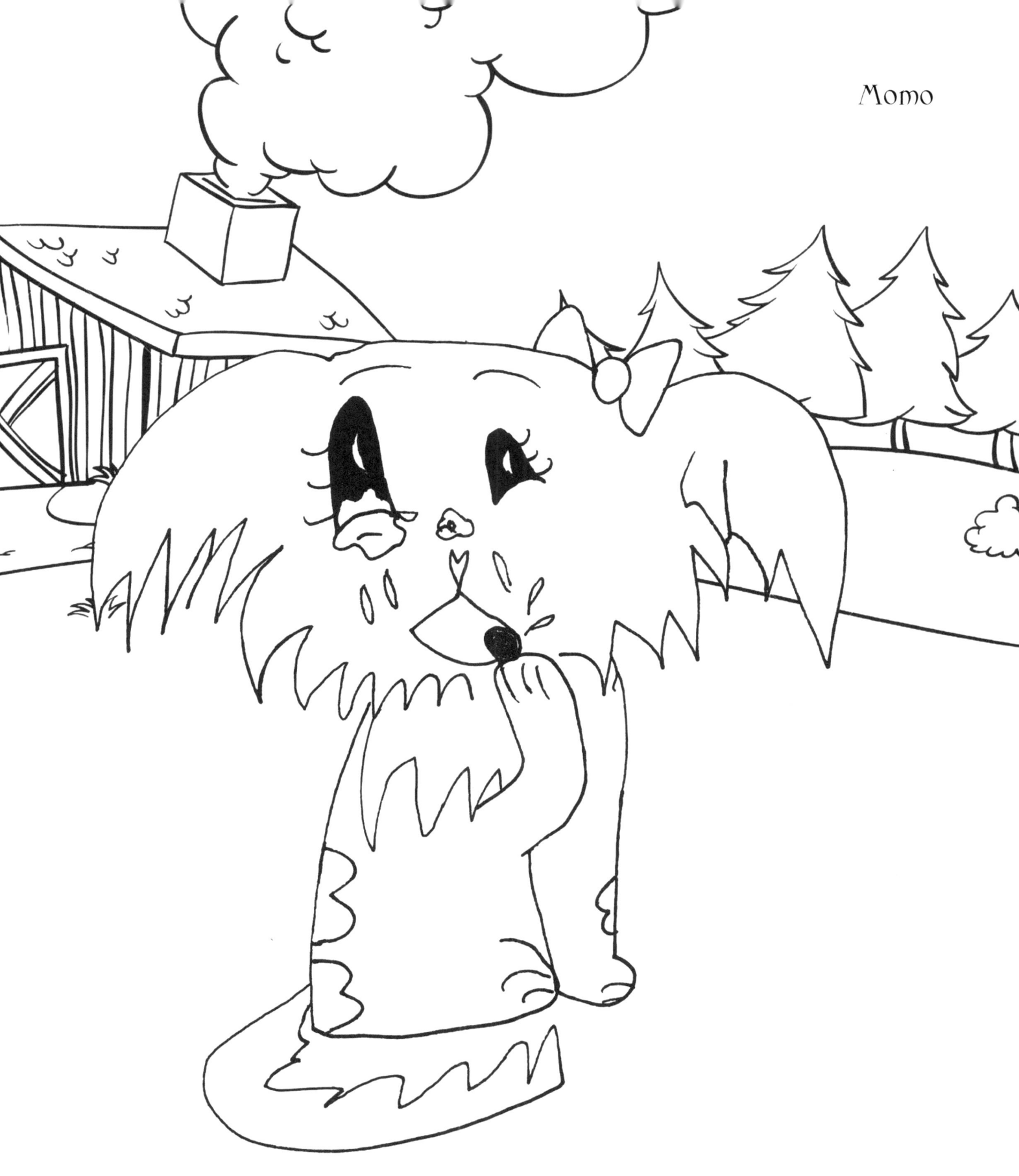

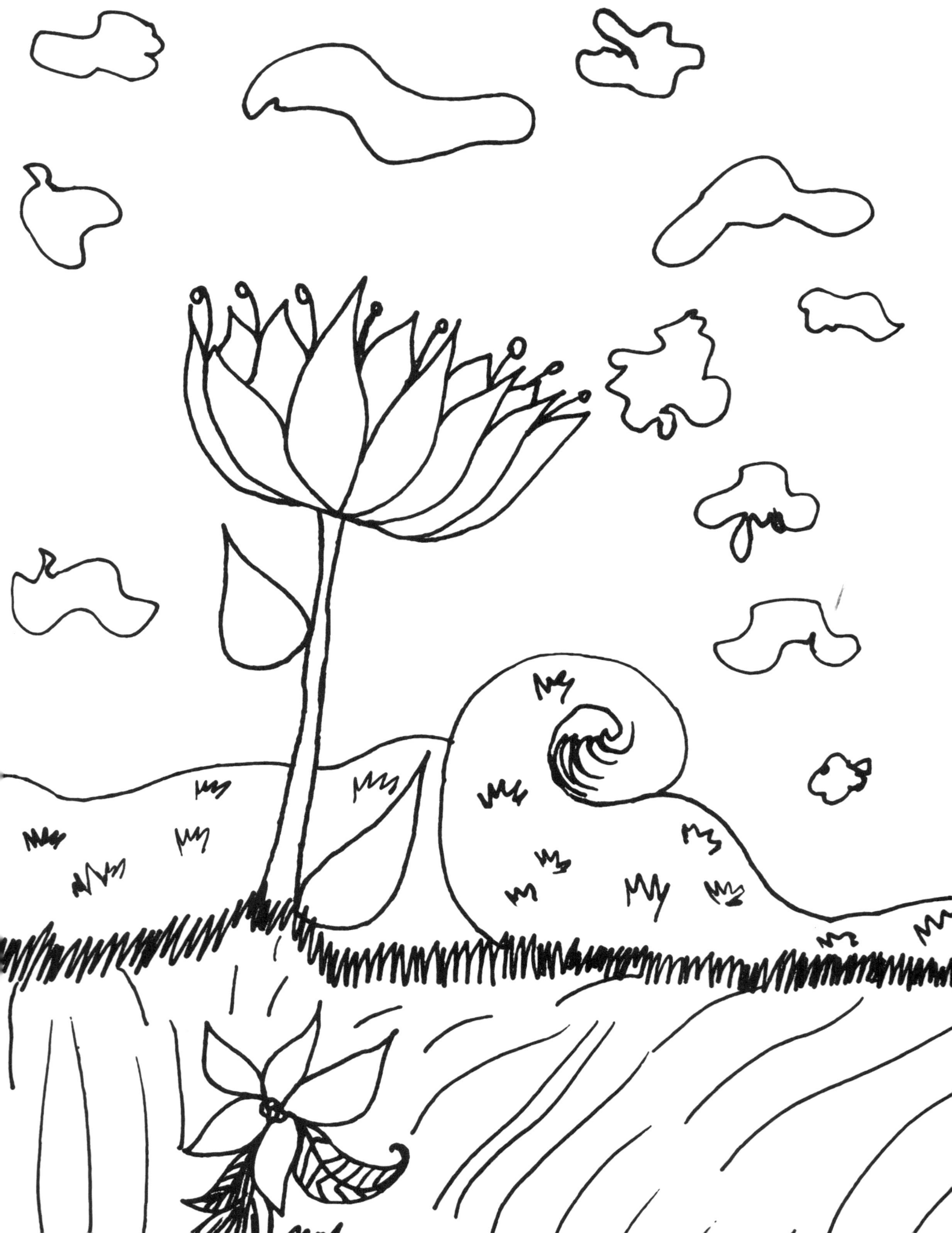

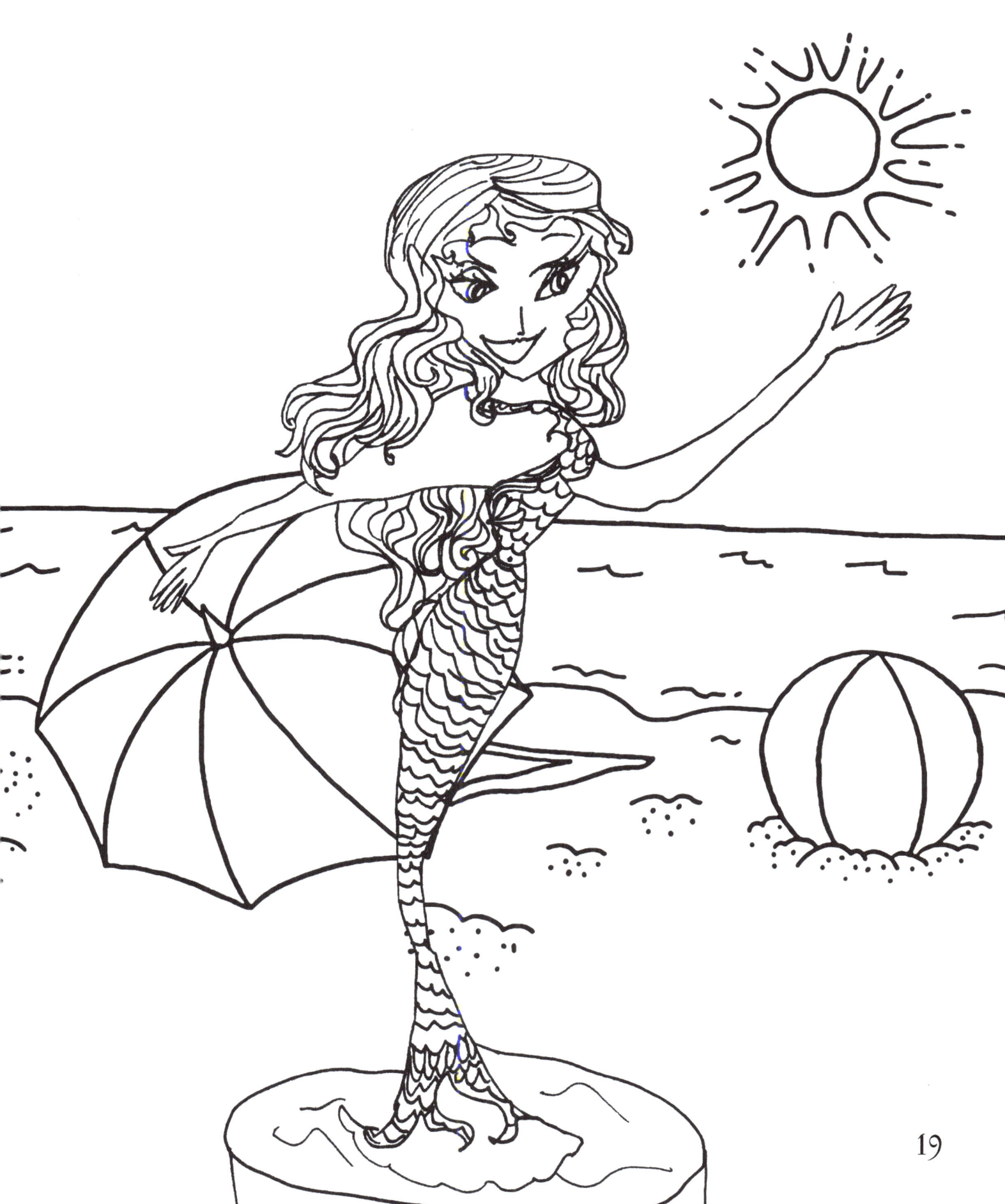

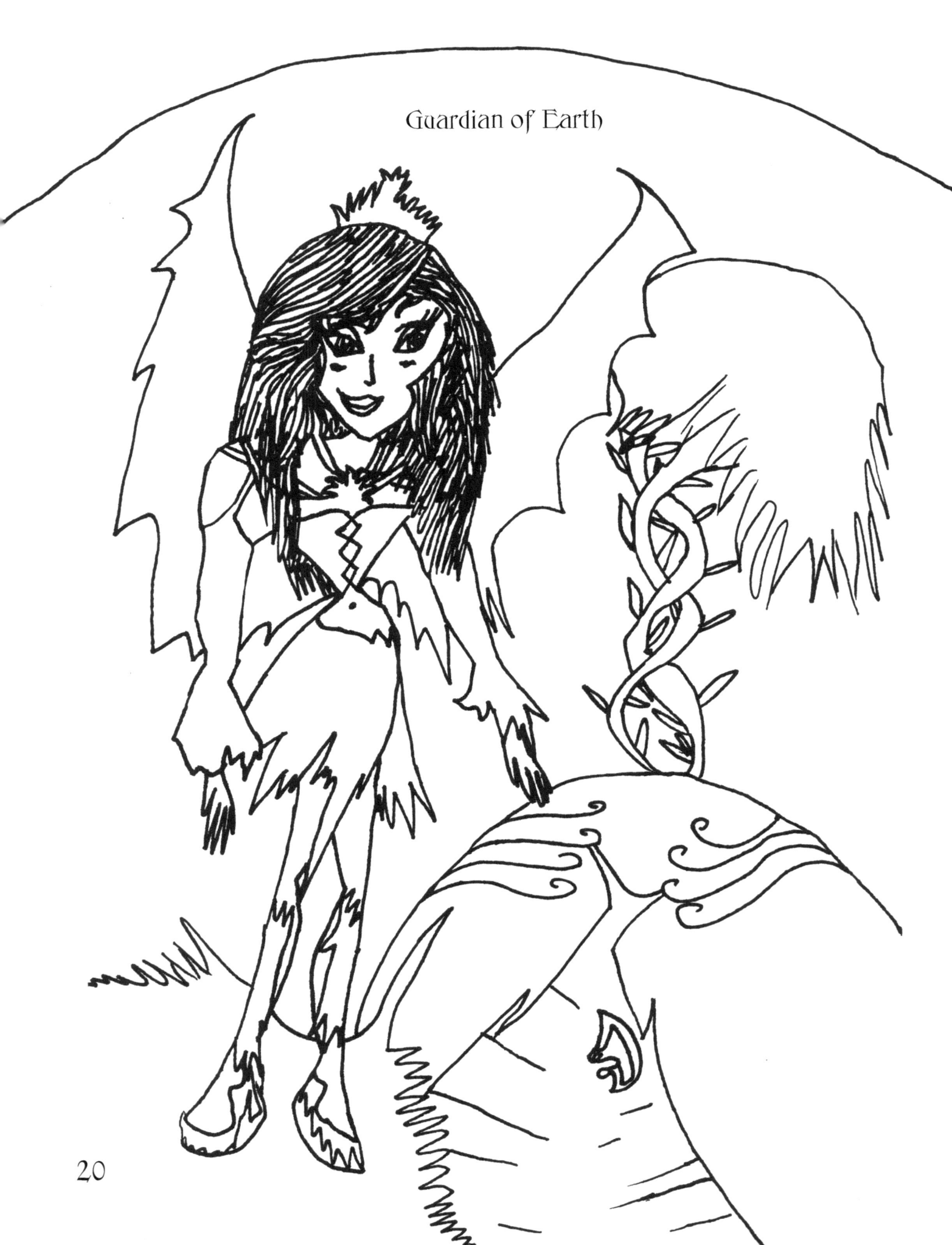

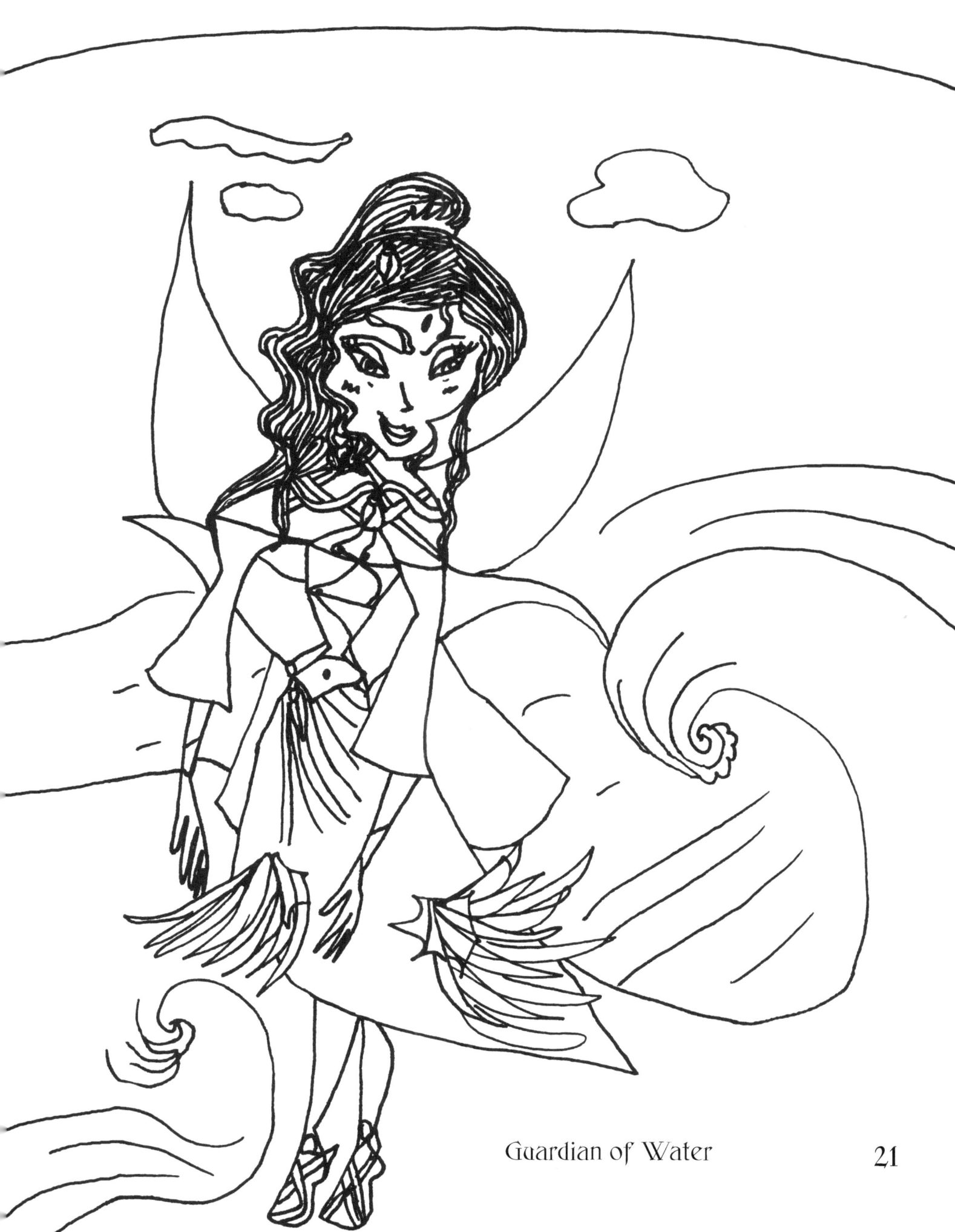

Guardian of Water

21

Rose

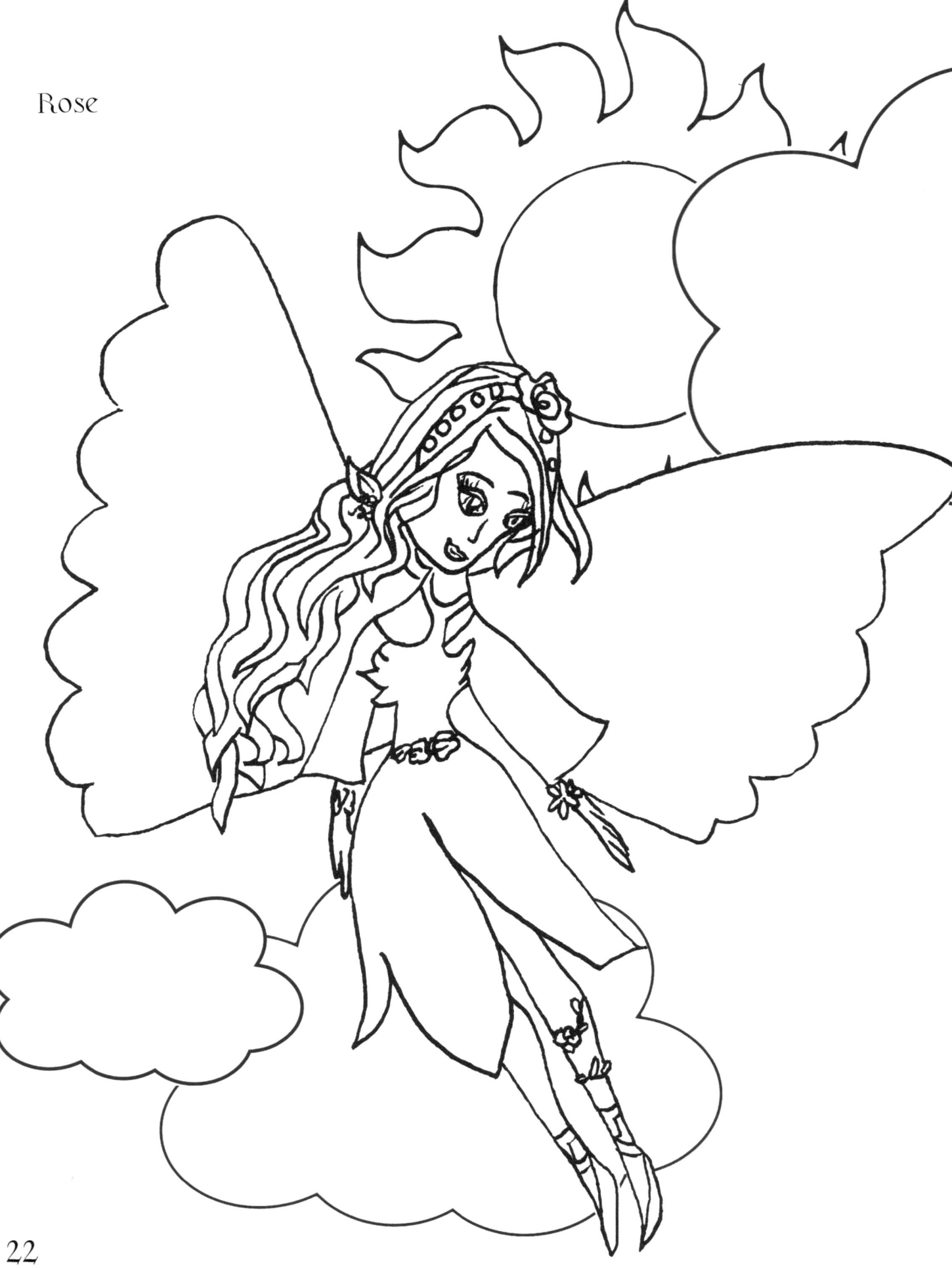

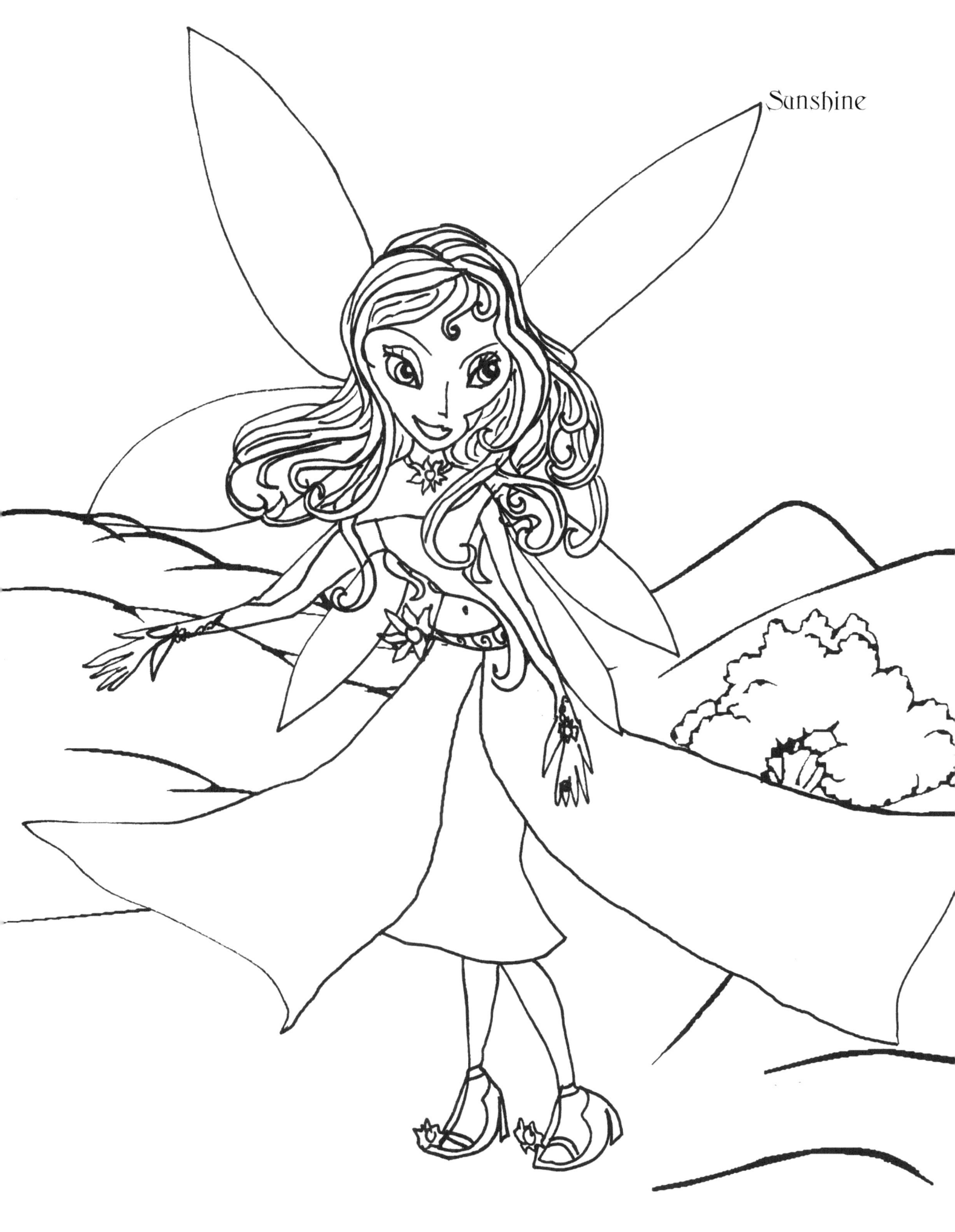

Sanshine

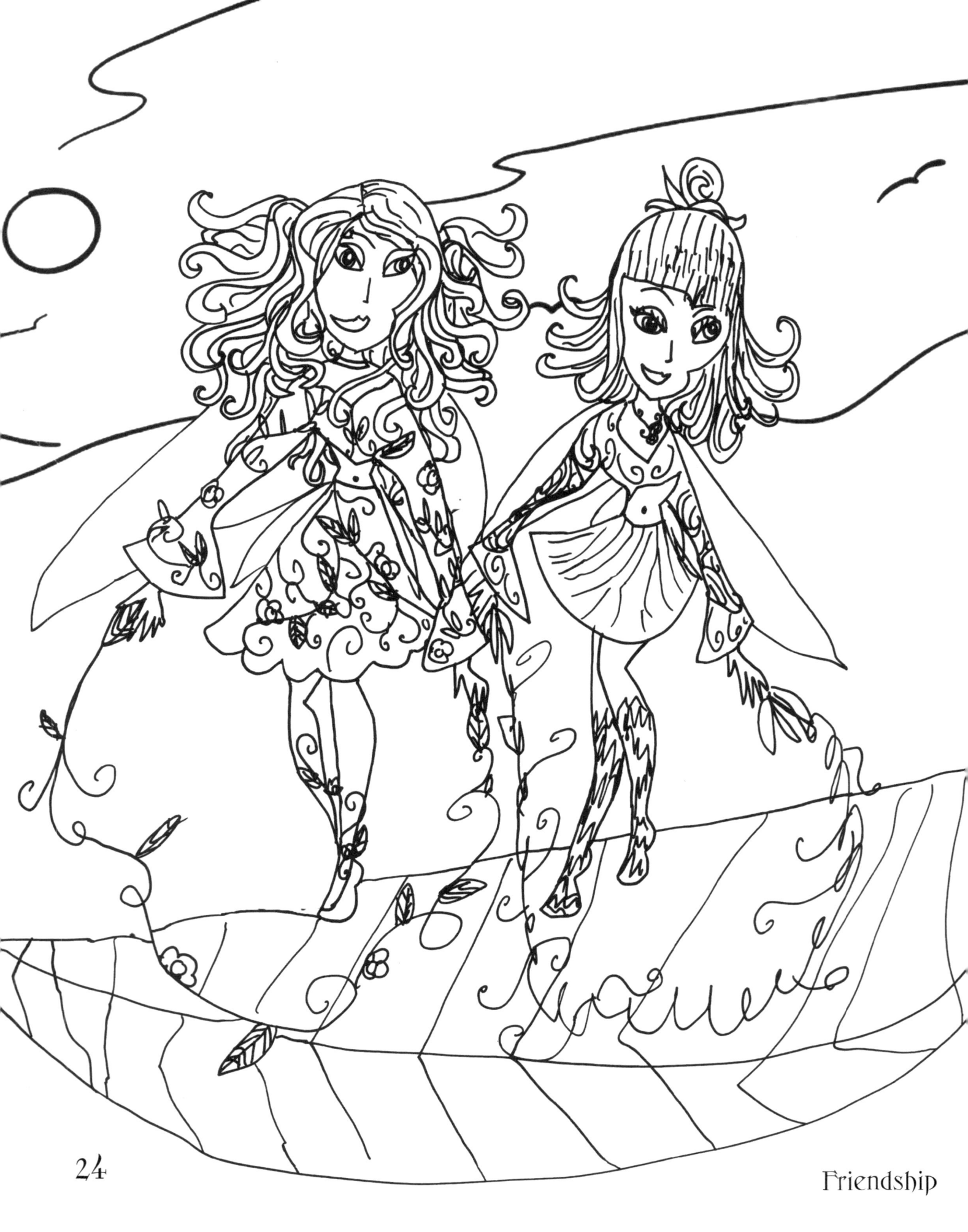

Friendship

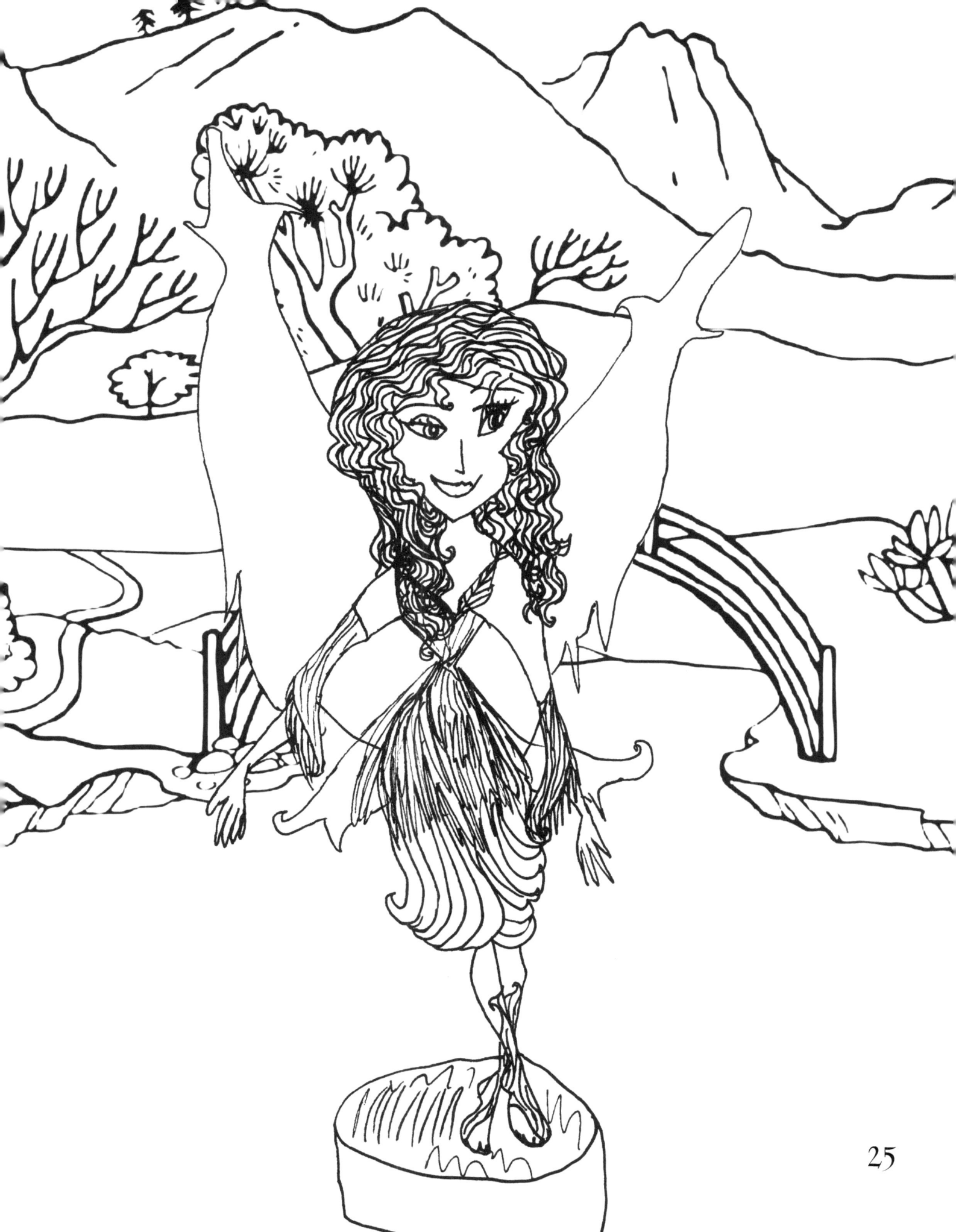

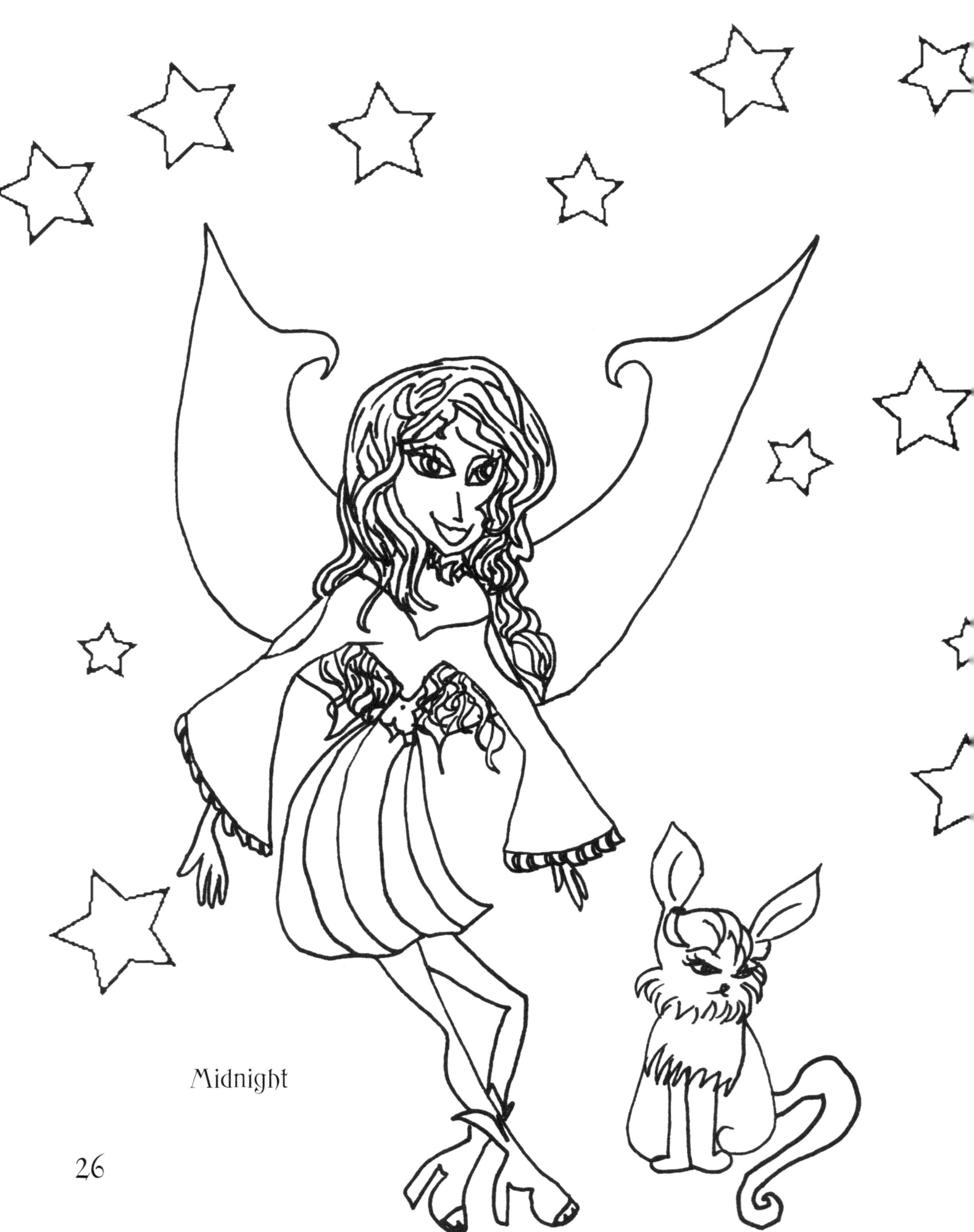

Midnight

26

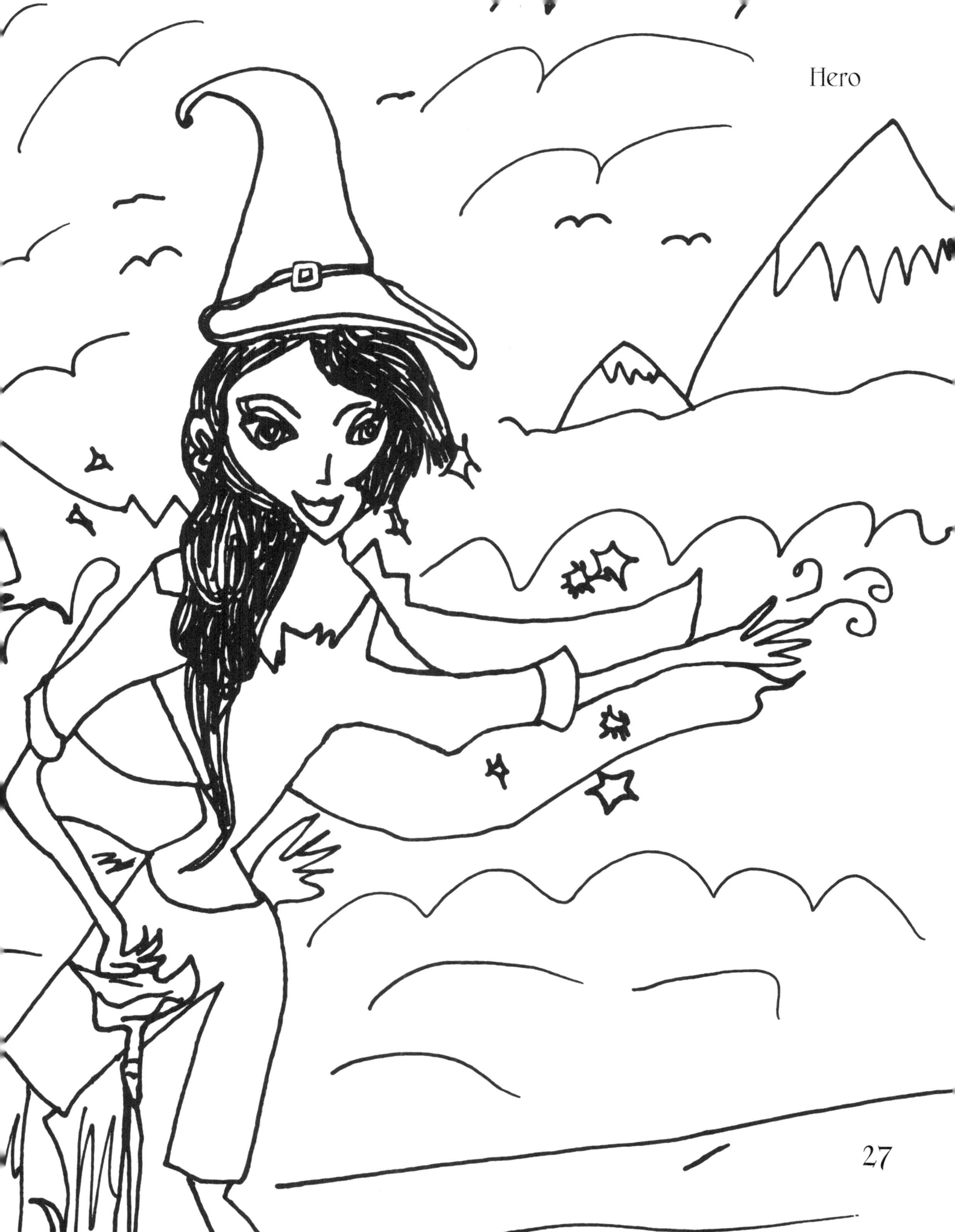

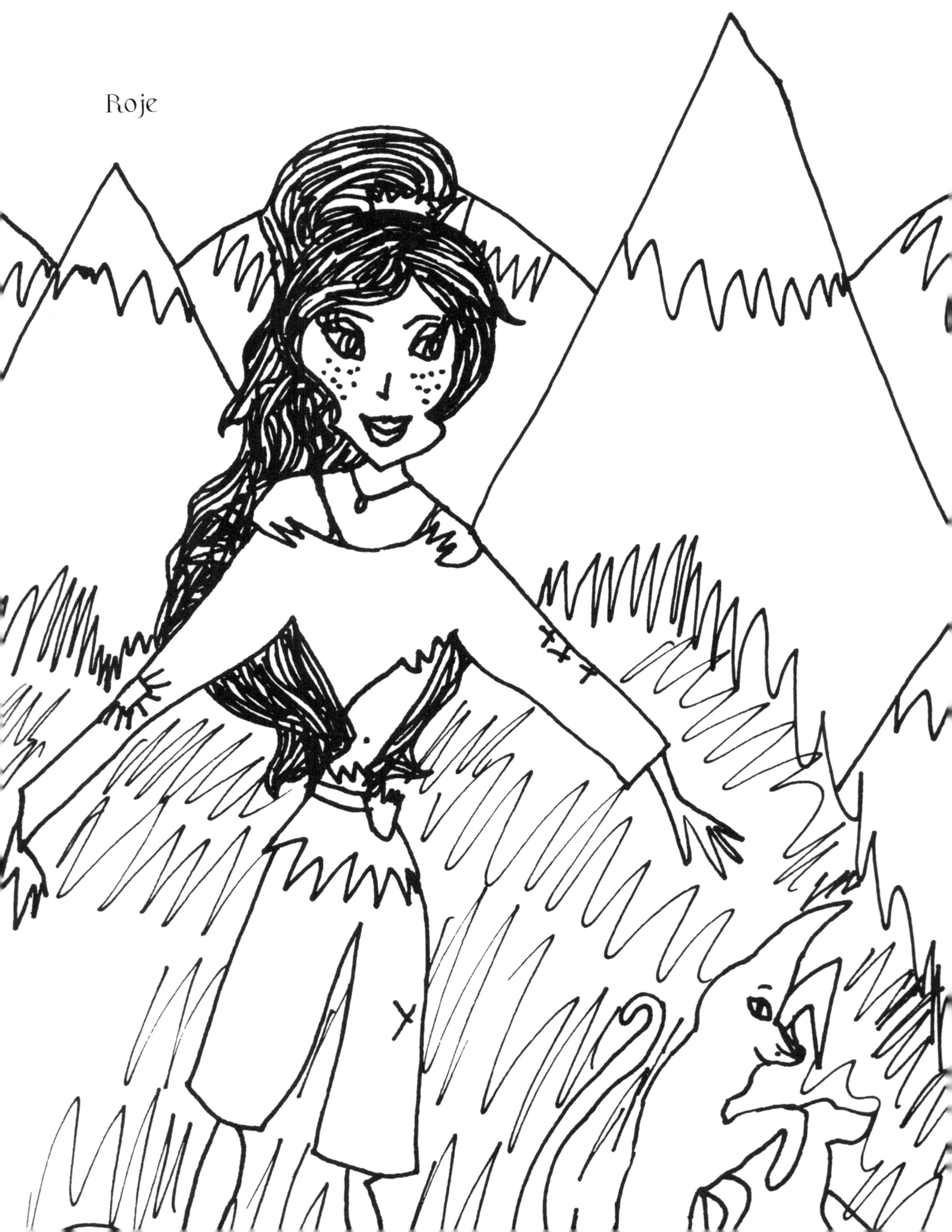

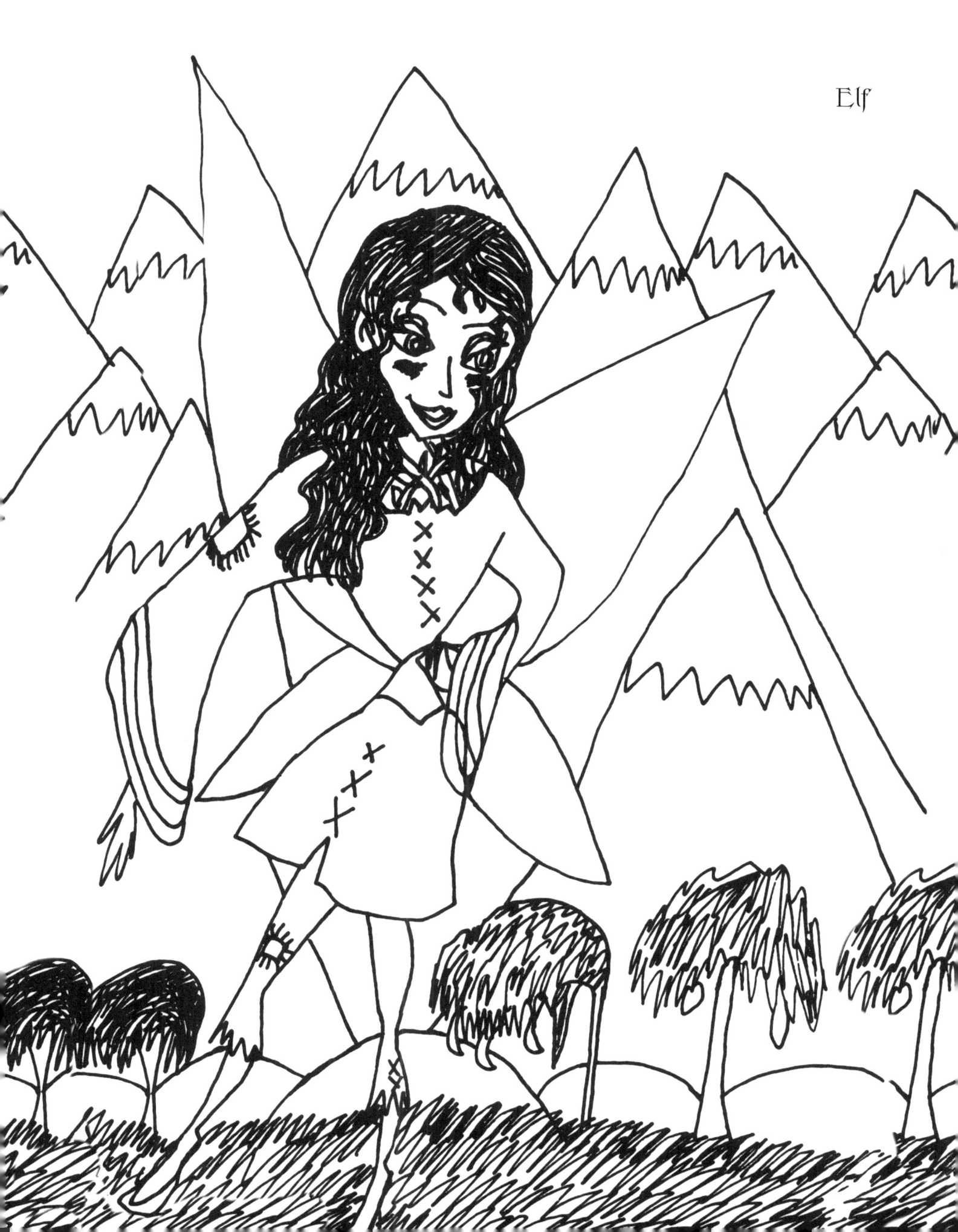

Elf

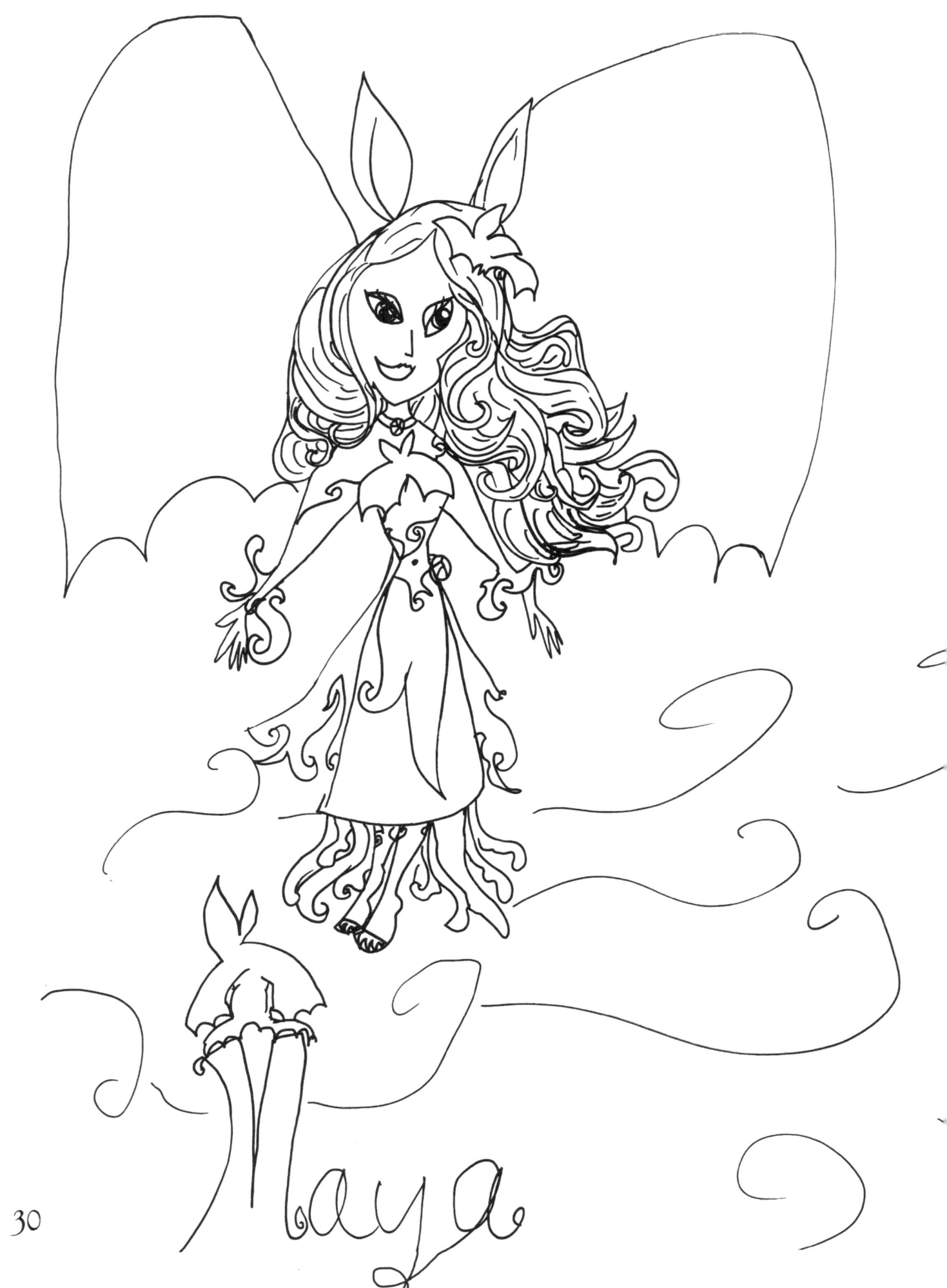

WHY I MADE THIS BOOK

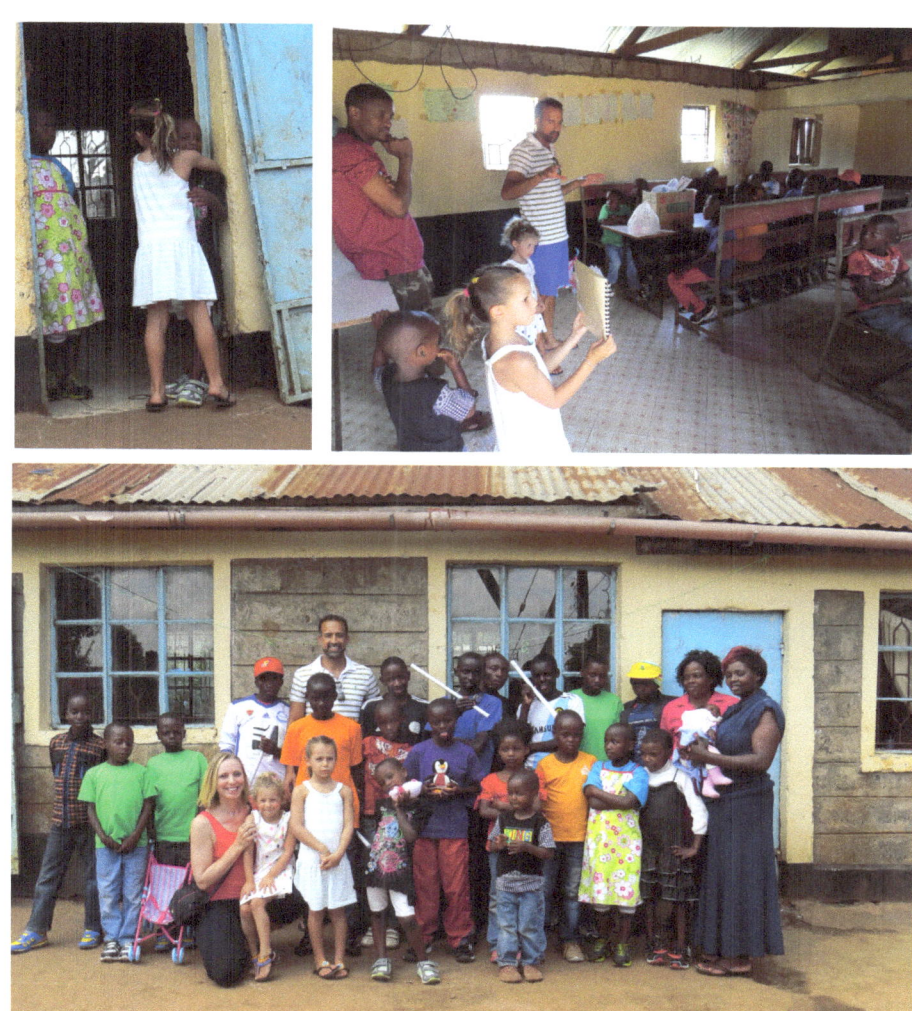

I created this coloring book to raise money for the orphans in Kenya and to help buy them food and go to school. When I visited them in 2015, I made friends there and I saw how little they had. They don t have much drawing paper and pens so I brought them some with my family. Thank you for buying my coloring book and helping to make money for the orphans.

Love, Maya

www.ingramcontent.com/pod-product-compliance
Lightning Source LLC
Chambersburg PA
CBHW050419180526

45159CB00005B/2329